READING/WRITING
COMPANION

Mc
Graw
Hill
Education

Cover: Nathan Love, Erwin Madrid

mheducation.com/prek-12

Copyright © McGraw-Hill Education

Send all inquiries to:
McGraw-Hill Education
Two Penn Plaza
New York, NY 10121

ISBN: 978-0-07-901846-5
MHID: 0-07-901846-7

Printed in the United States of America.

11 LMN 23

D

Welcome to Wonders!

Read exciting **Literature**, **Science**, and **Social Studies** texts!

★ **LEARN** about the world around you!

★ **THINK, SPEAK,** and **WRITE** about genres!

★ **COLLABORATE** in discussions and inquiry!

★ **EXPRESS** yourself!

my.mheducation.com

Use your student login to read texts and practice phonics, spelling, grammar, and more!

Unit 1 Getting to Know Us

Start Smart

The Big Idea
What makes you special? 18

Week 1 • At School

Digital Tools *Find this eBook and other resources at:* **my.mheducation.com**

Week 2 • Where I Live

Week 3 • Our Pets

Week 4 • Let's Be Friends

Blend Images/Alamy

Week 5 • Let's Move!

Writing and Grammar

Wrap Up the Unit

We Are All Readers

My Favorite Books

 Talk about what these children like to read about.

 Share what you know about one of these topics.

I like reading this book because it is about . . .

Talk about your favorite books.

 Draw and **write** about one of your favorite books.

My Story

Everybody has a story.
Your story starts with you.

 Introduce yourself to your partner.

 Draw yourself and **write** your name.

_____

- -

_____

Draw and **write** what you like best about yourself.

A **nursery rhyme** is a short poem or song for children. It can have words that rhyme.

 Listen to "l, 2, Buckle My Shoe."

 Act out the actions of the rhyme in order. Say what you are doing.

 Number each picture in the correct order.

_____

_____

Say the directions for your partner to act out.

Tell your partner three actions to act out. Say each direction while you act it out.

Draw your actions in the correct order.

 Follow your partner's directions.

A **fairy tale** is a story about magical characters and made-up places.

 Listen to "Jack and the Beanstalk."

Talk about how you know this is a fairy tale.

Draw or **write** about what makes this story a fairy tale.

Nonfiction tells about real people, places, and things.

Listen to "Work, Play, and Learn Together."

Talk about what makes this a nonfiction text.

Write two real things this text is about.

1.

2.

Unit 1
Getting to Know Us

Listen to the poem, "Something About Me."

Look at the girl bending down in the picture. Talk about the ways she is growing.

Draw a star next to something the girl is doing that you can do.

CHOOL BUS

The Big Idea
What makes you special?

Essential Question What do you do at your school?

Talk about what these girls are doing in school.

 Write or **draw** two things that you do at school.

wen

hei

Shared Read

Find Text Evidence

 Read to find out what Jack can do.

Point to each word in the title as you read it.

Essential Question

? What do you do at your school?

Jack Can

Shared Read

 Find Text Evidence

Circle and read aloud each word with short *a* as in *cat*.

Talk about what Max and Jack can do.

(Max) can.

Can Jack? Jack can.

Shared Read

 Find Text Evidence

Underline and read aloud the word *not*.

Talk about page 27. Picture in your mind how Jack's face might look.

Max can. Can Jack?

Jack can not.

 Find Text Evidence

✏ Circle and read aloud each word with short *a* as in *cat*.

✏ Underline and read aloud the words *what* and *does*.

Jack is sad.

Realistic Fiction

What does Nan do?

Shared Read

 Find Text Evidence

 Picture Jack's face when Nan helps. Talk about what you picture.

Retell the story using the pictures.

Nan helps Jack!

Jack likes school.

Realistic fiction is a genre. Realistic fiction stories are made up. They have characters that do things that could happen in real life.

Jack Can

 Reread to find out what makes this story realistic fiction.

 Share how you know it is realistic fiction.

Write the names of two characters. Then write something they each do that could happen in real life.

Who Could Be Real?	What Could Really Happen?
Jack	every thing

Key details are the most important details in a story. Words and pictures in a story give you the key details.

 Reread "Jack Can."

 Talk about key details in the story. Use the words and pictures.

 Write the key details.

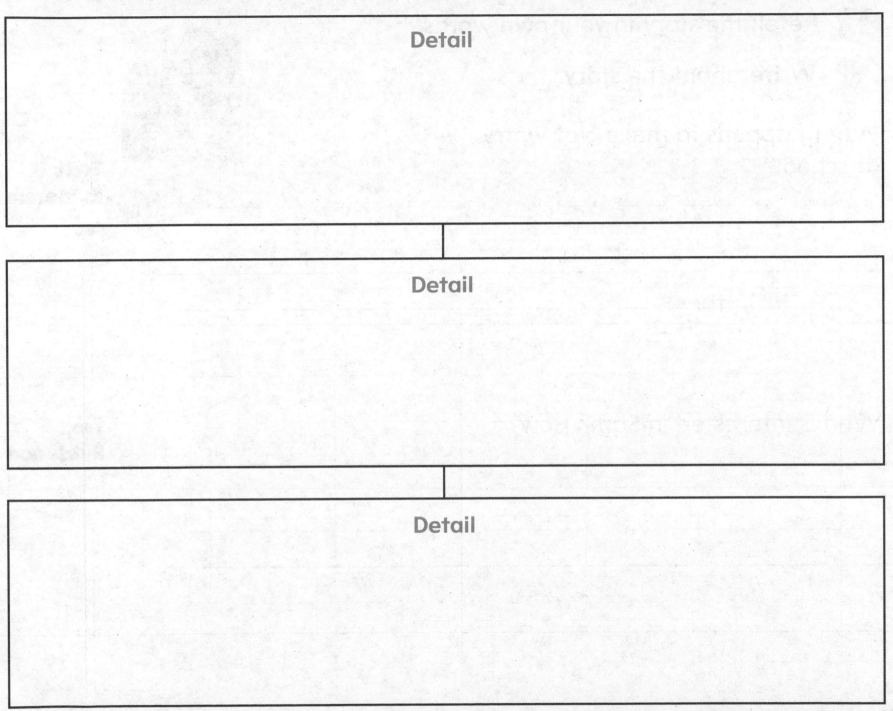

Detail

Detail

Detail

Retell the story in your own words.

Write about the story.

What happens to make Nat worry
at school?

Text Evidence

Page

_____

- -

_____

- -

_____

Who is interested in Sam? How?

Text Evidence

Page

_____

- -

_____

- -

_____

 Talk about how the stories are the same and different.

 Write about the stories.

How are Nat and Jack alike?

_____

_____

_____

_____

_____

How are you like Nat or Jack?

_____

_____

_____

_____

> **Quick Tip**
>
> Think how Nat and Jack are the same.
>
> *Nat and Jack both go to _____.*
>
> *Nat and Jack both like _____.*

Talk about what Nat is doing on pages 8–11.

 Write clues from the story that answer the questions.

What does Nat bring to school?	How can you tell Nat knows he should not do this?

How do you know how Nat feels at school?

_____

- -

_____

- -

_____

Talk about how Nat feels on page 12.

 Write about how the words and pictures help you understand how Nat feels.

How does Nat look?	What in the text tells you how strongly Nat feels?

How does Nat feel?

_____

- -

_____

- -

_____

Reread **Anchor Text**

 Talk about what Nat is doing and feeling on pages 15–17.

 Write what Nat does and how he feels.

What Nat Does	How Nat Feels

How have Nat's feelings about school changed?

_____

- -

_____

- -

_____

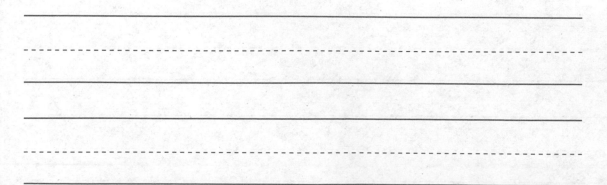

Write About It

How does the author help you understand how Nat's feelings about school change?

Rules at School

Why do we have rules at school?
Rules can help us get along.
Rules can help us stay safe.

Read to find out why we have rules at school.

Talk about what the children in the photo are doing.

Underline clues that tell why we have rules at school.

Purestock/SuperStock

We raise our hands.
We listen quietly.
We obey safety rules.
We let everyone play!
What are your school rules?

 Underline the rules that help us get along.

 Circle the rules that keep us safe.

 Talk about why rules at school are important.

Ariel Skelley/Blend Images/Getty Images

Quick Tip

Photos can show you what the text means.

Talk about what you learn about rules from the text.

Write what the photos and words teach you about rules at school.

Photos	Words

Why did the author use the title "Rules at School?"

_____

- -

_____

- -

_____

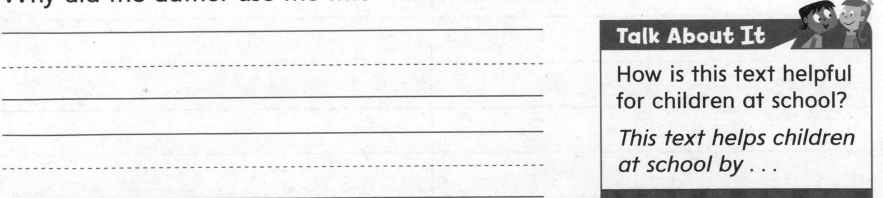

Talk About It

How is this text helpful for children at school?

This text helps children at school by . . .

Class Poll

Step 1 Write a question about things your classmates like to do best at school.

_____

_____

_____

_____

Step 2 List five things to do at school.

Favorite Things	Number of Children
1.	
2.	
3.	
4.	
5.	

Step 3 Decide how many classmates you will poll.

Step 4 Ask your classmates to take your poll. Use the chart to tally how many like each thing best.

Step 5 Think about the results of your poll. What did you learn about your classmates?

_____

_____

_____

_____

_____

Talk about what this song is about.

 Talk about why the "ABC Song" is good to sing. Tell your partner how that makes the "ABC Song" like "Jack Can."

ABC Song

A B C D E F G

H I J K L M N O P

Q R S T U V

W X Y and Z

Now I know my ABC's.

Next time won't you

sing with me?

2HotBrazil/E+/Getty Images

What I Know Now

Think about the texts you heard and read this week about school. Write what you learned.

_____

- -

_____

- -

_____

- -

_____

 Think about what else you would like to learn about school. Talk about your ideas.

 Share one thing you learned this week about realistic fiction stories.

Talk and ask questions about what this boy sees outside his window.

 Share something you see outside where you live. Write or draw what you see.

Shared Read

🔍 **Find Text Evidence**

 Read to find out what an animal family does where they live.

 Point to each word in the title as you read it.

Essential Question

? What is it like where you live?

Six Kids

Shared Read

 Find Text Evidence

Underline and read aloud the words *out* and *up*.

Think about what the family is going to do. Tell what you picture.

Six kids go out.

Six kids go up a hill.

Shared Read

 Find Text Evidence

 Underline and read aloud the word *down*.

Circle and read aloud each word with short *i* as in *pig*.

Six kids dig, dig, dig.

Six kids go down.

Shared Read

 Find Text Evidence

 **Talk** about why the kids are very blue.

 Circle and read aloud the words with short *i* as in *pig.*

Six kids pick, pick, pick.

Six kids are very blue.

Shared Read

Find Text Evidence

 Picture the chicks before and after they swim. How are they different?

Retell the story using the words and pictures.

Six kids dip, dip, dip.

That will fix it.

Six kids like it here!

Fantasy is a genre. A fantasy is a made-up story. It has characters, a setting, or events that could not happen in real life.

 Reread to find out what makes this a fantasy.

 Share how you know it is a fantasy.

Write two events from the story that show it is a fantasy.

What Happens	Why It Could Not Happen in Real Life

Remember, key details are the most important details in a story. Key details happen in order, or in sequence.

 Reread "Six Kids."

 Talk about the sequence of the key details.

 Write key details about what the six kids do. Write the details in order.

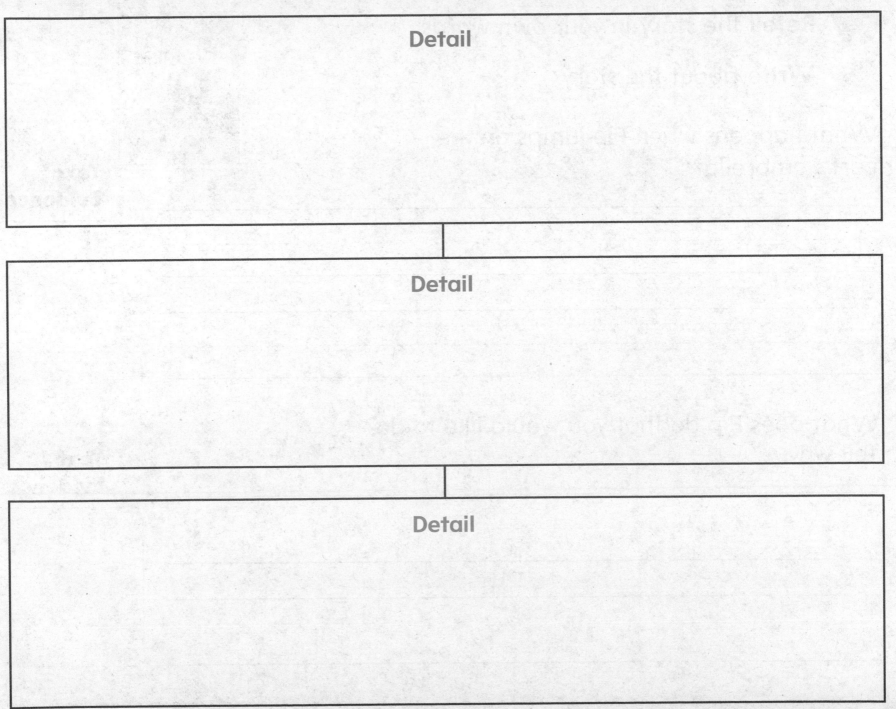

Detail

Detail

Detail

👥 **Retell** the story in your own words.

✏️ **Write** about the story.

Go, Pip!
by Tomek Bogacki

What happens when Pip jumps on the cart's umbrella?

🔍 **Text Evidence**

Page

What does Pip do that you would like to do? Tell why.

🔍 **Text Evidence**

Page

Talk about how the stories are the same and different.

Write about the stories.

How are the chicks and Pip alike?

_____

- - - - - - - - - - - - - - - - - - - -

_____

- - - - - - - - - - - - - - - - - - - -

_____

How is where the chicks live and where Pip lives different?

_____

- - - - - - - - - - - - - - - - - - - -

_____

- - - - - - - - - - - - - - - - - - - -

_____

Combine Information

Reread each story to find out how the chicks and Pip are alike.

In the end, Pip feels . . .

In the end, the chicks feel . . .

Where I Live **65**

Talk about how the people feel about Pip on page 31.

 Write two clues that tell how Pip and the people are feeling on pages 30–31.

1.	2.

What does the author want to show on these pages?

_____

_____

_____

_____

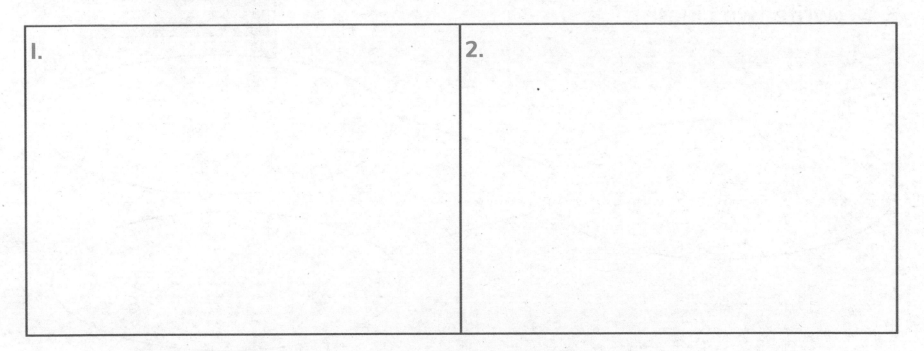

Talk about what Pip is doing on pages 32–35.

Write two clues that show you what Pip likes to do in the city.

1.	2.

How do you know Pip wants to visit new places?

_____

- -

_____

_____

- -

_____

Talk about what Pip is doing on pages 36–39.

Write how Pip is feeling. Then write two clues.

Pip feels

Why is *Go, Pip!* a good title for this story?

_____

_____

_____

Write About It

Describe how where Pip lives affects what he does.

A Surprise in the City

Hi! My name is Zoë. I live in the city. Mom has a surprise for me today.

Mom takes me to the swings. Is **this** my surprise? Mom says no.

 Read to find out about Zoë's surprise.

 Circle the words that Zoë uses to talk about herself.

 Talk about the bold word *this*. What does it tell you about how Zoë speaks?

Mom buys me a pretzel.
Is **this** my surprise?
Mom says no.

Mom stops at the pencil store.
This is my surprise!
I buy pencils.
I **love** my surprise!

Underline the words that repeat from page 69.

Talk about how this builds excitement in the story.

Quick Tip

Words in bold print can tell you what is important.

Talk about Zoë. Describe what you learn about her from the story.

 Write two things you learn about Zoë.

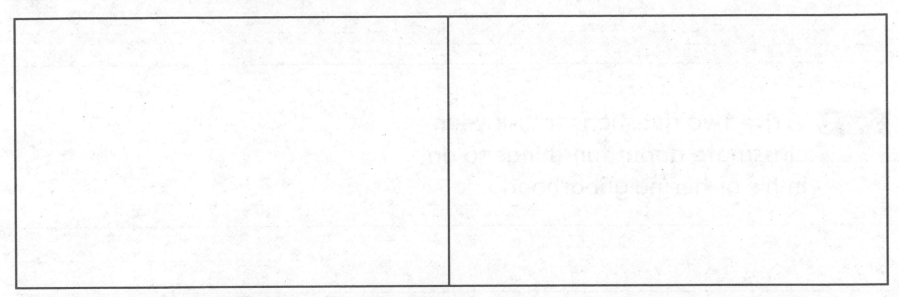

How does the author let you know Zoë's thoughts and feelings?

_____

- - - - - - - - - - - - - - - - - - - -

_____

_____

- - - - - - - - - - - - - - - - - - - -

_____

Write About It

Write about an event that happened to you.

Use words that help readers know you are telling about yourself.

Fun in Our Neighborhoods

Step 1 Find a classmate to interview.

_____

- - - - - - - - - - - - - - - - - - - -

_____

Step 2 Write two questions to ask your
classmate about fun things to do
in his or her neighborhood.

_____

- - - - - - - - - - - - - - - - - - - -

_____

- - - - - - - - - - - - - - - - - - - -

_____

- - - - - - - - - - - - - - - - - - - -

_____

Step 3 Interview your classmate.

Step 4 Write the answers to your questions.

_____

- -

_____

- -

_____

- -

_____

- -

_____

Step 5 Draw your classmate doing the activity.

Step 6 Choose how to present your work.

Make Connections

 Talk about what the people in the picture are doing.

 Compare how this picture and the pictures in "Six Kids" are alike.

People like to spend time in parks.

What I Know Now

Think about the texts you heard and read this week about places where people live. Write what you learned.

_____

- -

_____

_____

- -

_____

_____

- -

_____

 Think about a place you would like to learn more about. Talk about your ideas.

 Share one thing you learned this week about fantasy stories.

Talk About It

Essential Question **What makes a pet special?**

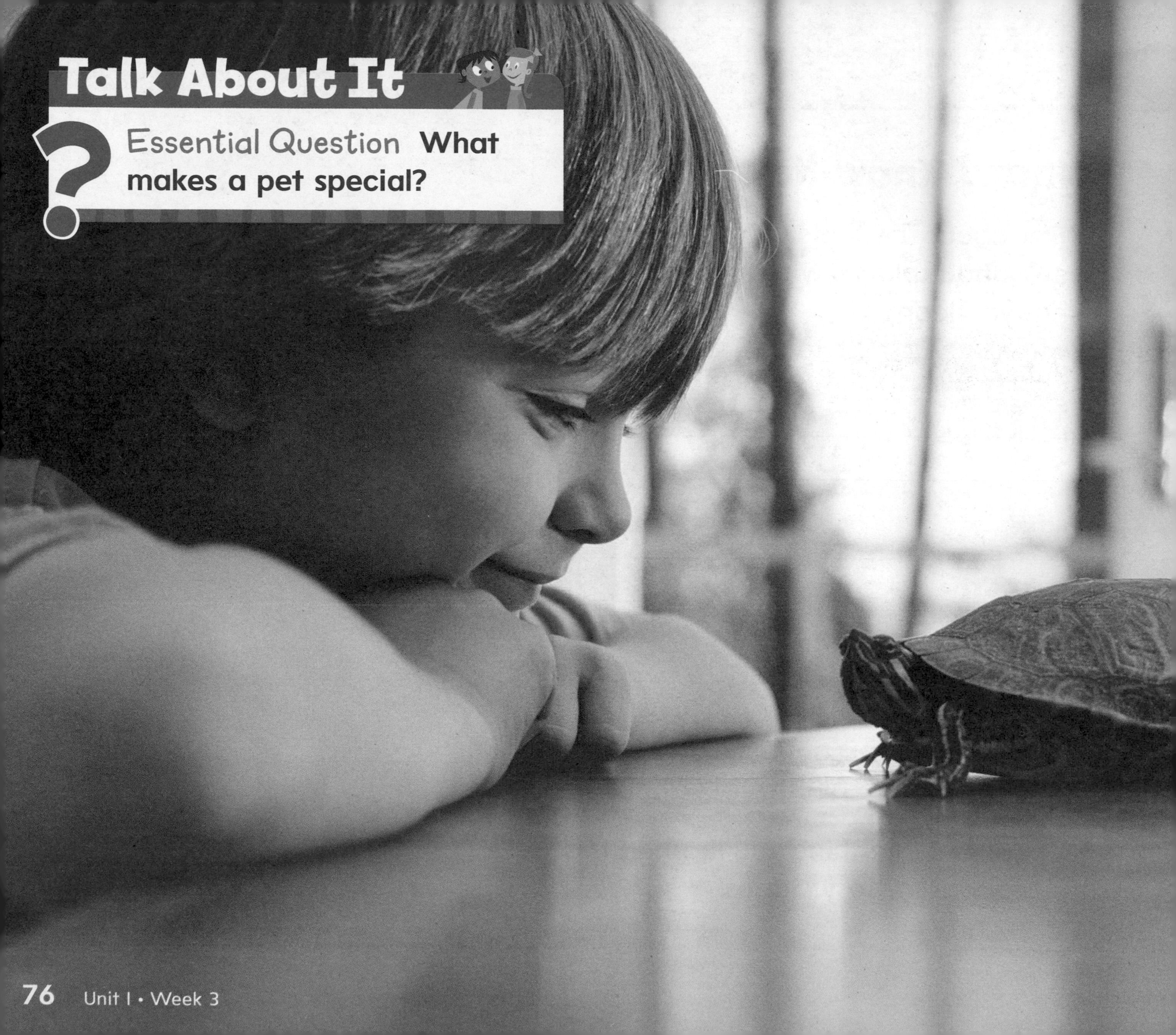

Talk and ask questions about what makes this turtle special.

 Write about what makes pets special.

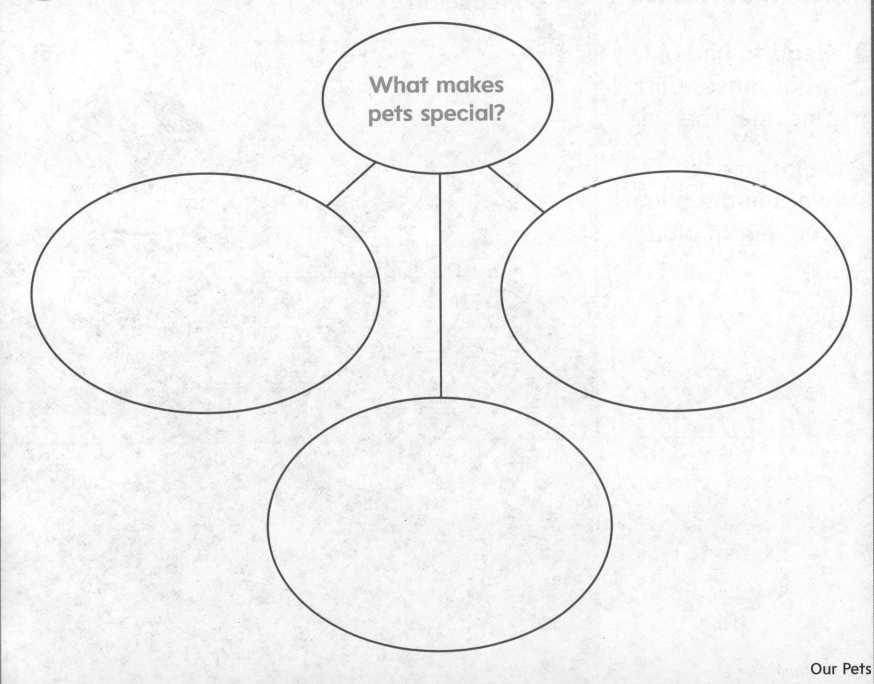

What makes pets special?

Andersen Ross/Stockbyte/Getty Images

Shared Read

Find Text Evidence

 Read to find out what makes Cliff Cat's pet special.

 Point to each word in the title as you read it aloud.

Essential Question

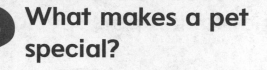 What makes a pet special?

A Pig for Cliff

Find Text Evidence

Circle and read aloud the words that have the same beginning sounds as *click*.

 **Talk** about why Slim is a funny name for the pig.

Cliff Cat is glad.

Cliff Cat has a new pet.

It is Slim.

Slim is a big black pig.

Shared Read

 Find Text Evidence

Underline and read aloud the word *come*.

Talk about how you picture Slim's face on these pages. Tell why.

Slim can not fit in!

Come out, Slim!

🔍 **Find Text Evidence**

 Circle and read aloud the words that have the same beginning sounds as *slick*.

Talk about why Slim cannot sit with Cliff Cat.

Slam!

Cliff Cat can not sit in it with Slim.

Cliff Cat and Slim slip.

Find Text Evidence

 Underline and read aloud the words *pull, be,* and *good.*

 Retell the story using the words and pictures.

Slim can go up a hill.

Cliff Cat can not.

Slim can pull Cliff Cat.

Slim will be a good pet!

Remember, a fantasy is a made-up story. It has characters that could not come from real life.

 Reread to find out about the characters.

 Talk about why the characters could not be real.

 Write how the characters show the story is a fantasy.

Characters	Why They Could Not Be Real

Remember, key details are the most important details in a story. Key details happen in sequence, or in order.

 Reread "A Pig for Cliff."

 Talk about the sequence of the key details.

Write key details about what Cliff Cat and Slim do. Write the details in order.

Detail

Pig Cliff the cat got a

Detail

When they tried to swing brove

Detail

Slim can Pull Cliff

Retell the story in your own words.

Write about the story.

Why does Flip have to sneak into class?

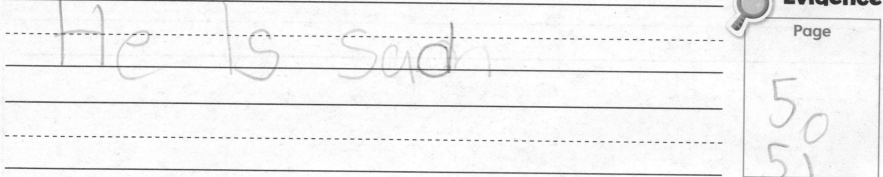

He is sad

Text Evidence

Page

5 0
51

Why is Flip glad in the end?

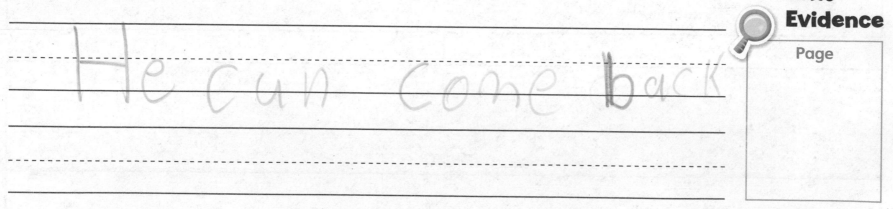

He can come back

Text Evidence

Page

Talk about how the stories are the same and different.

 Write about the stories.

How are Slim and Flip both able to help?

Slim tabps pu
and so dcer flip.

How are Flip and Slim different from other classroom pets?

They are
laraer.

Make Inferences

Use details to figure out things that are not told in the story.

Flip helps by . . .
Slim helps by . . .

Talk about what you learn about Flip and the girl on pages 51–54.

Write a clue from the story that answers the question.

How does Flip get into the school?

Fiip Pull the

girl tin

Why does the girl tell Flip to be good?

to beep gidn

st

Talk about what is happening on pages 58–60.

 Write clues from the story that tell about Miss Black and Flip.

What is Miss Black's problem?	What does Flip do?
She can V R en	He hame pq yt twr.

How does the author help you know Flip's plan?

hie cvs are big.

Talk about how you know Miss Black's feelings have changed on page 61.

Write clues from the story that tell how Miss Black feels.

Beginning	End

Why did Miss Black change her mind about Flip?

_____

- -

_____

- -

Write About It

In your writer's notebook, write a story about what happens when you take a make-believe pet to school.

What Pets Need

What do pets need?
Like all living things, pets
need food.
Some pets eat seeds or plants.

 Read to find out what pets need.

 Underline the word that tells you what pets need.

Talk about what the photo shows. How do you know what animal it is?

hamster

Juniors Bildarchiv/age fotostock

Some pets eat meat or fish.
All pets need fresh water.
Pets need a safe home.
Pets need our love
and care.

Underline the words that tell what pets need.

Circle the label. Talk about what kittens need.

kittens

Quick Tip

Labels give information about what you see in the photos.

Talk about the question the author asks on page 97.

 Write the answers to the question and where you find them.

Page	What do pets need?

Why is "What Pets Need" a good title?

_____

- -

_____

- -

_____

Talk About It

How does the author show what pets need?

The author helps by using . . .

Plan for a Pet's Home

Step 1 **Pick** a type of classroom pet.

_____

- -

_____

Step 2 **Write** questions about the home your classroom pet needs.

_____

- -

_____

- -

_____

- -

_____

Step 3 **Find** books to answer your questions. Use the tables of contents to find information.

Step 4 **Write** the answers to your questions.

_____

- -

_____

- -

_____

- -

_____

Step 5 **Draw** what your pet's home in the classroom will look like.

Step 6 **Choose** how to present your work.

Make Connections

✏️ **Circle** two words that Owl uses to tell Pussy that she is special to him.

👥 **Talk** about how the girl shows that Flip is special to her. How is her way different from Owl's way?

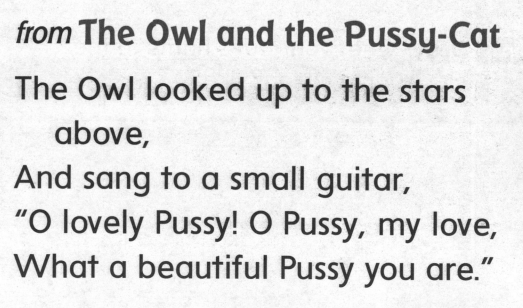

from **The Owl and the Pussy-Cat**

The Owl looked up to the stars
   above,
And sang to a small guitar,
"O lovely Pussy! O Pussy, my love,
What a beautiful Pussy you are."

— by Edward Lear

What I Know Now

Think about the texts you heard and read this week about pets. Write what you learned.

_____

- -

_____

- -

_____

- -

_____

 Think about what else you would like to learn about pets. Talk about your ideas.

 Share one thing you learned this week about fantasy stories.

Talk About It

Essential Question What do friends do together?

Talk about what these friends are doing.

Draw something you do with your friends.
Share how you feel about your friends.

Compassionate Eye Foundation/Tanya Constantine/Photodisc/Getty Images

Shared Read

Find Text Evidence

 Ask any questions you may have about the text. Read to find the answer.

Circle and read aloud the words with short *o* as in *fog*.

Essential Question

? What do friends do together?

Toss!
Kick!
Hop!

Shared Read

 Find Text Evidence

 Talk about what the text and pictures tell you about how kids play together.

Talk about what it means to "zip, zip, zip."

Kids play together.

Kids zip, zip, zip.

Shared Read

🔍 Find Text Evidence

 Underline and read aloud the word *too*.

Ask any questions you may have about the text. Read to find the answer.

Kids toss, toss, toss.

Kids kick, kick, kick, too!

Find Text Evidence

Circle and read aloud each word with short *o*.

Underline and read aloud the word *make*.

Kids make block houses.

Kids make dolls.

Shared Read

 Find Text Evidence

 Talk about what happens when a kid flops.

 **Retell** the text using the pictures and words from the text.

Kids hop in sacks.

Hop, hop, flop!

They have fun!

Nonfiction is a genre. A nonfiction text gives facts about real people and what they do. It may use photos.

 Reread to find out what makes this a nonfiction text.

 Share how you know it is nonfiction.

Write facts from two pages in the text using the words and photos.

Facts in Words and Photos

1.

fheoNunaircadreu

2.

ftaegosin

Key details tell important information about the text. Photos can give key details.

 Reread "Toss! Kick! Hop!"

 Talk about key details in the text. Use the words and photos.

Write key details about how friends play together.

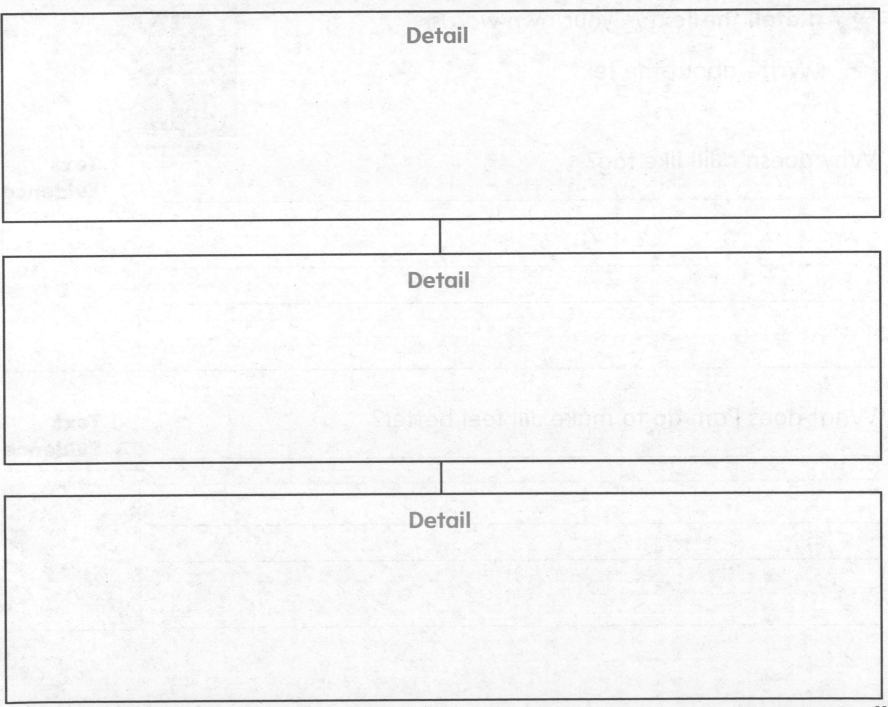

Detail

Detail

Detail

Retell the text in your own words.

Write about the text.

Friends
by Nina Crews

Why doesn't Jill like tag?

_____

- -

_____

- -

_____

Text Evidence

Page

What does Pam do to make Jill feel better?

_____

- -

_____

- -

_____

Text Evidence

Page

Talk about how the texts are the same and different.

 Write about the texts.

What do both texts tell about?

_____

_____

_____

_____

_____

What does *Friends* teach you about the way friends play together?

_____

_____

_____

_____

Combine Information

As you read, think about what you learn about friends.

At first I thought Jill and Pam _____.

Then I learned that they _____.

Share what Pam and Jill do together on pages 70–71.

Write clues from the text and photos that help you know what friends can do.

On pages 70–71, Pam and Jill...

How do you know what friends can do?

Talk about the girls' feelings on pages 72–75.

Write clues from the text that answer the questions.

What makes Pam happy?	What makes Jill unhappy?

What do the photos show you about how Pam and Jill are different?

_____

- -

_____

_____

- -

_____

Talk about how you know Pam and Jill are good friends on pages 76–79.

 Write clues from the text that help you know that Pam is a good friend to Jill.

Clues

Why does Pam think of something else to do?

_____

_____

_____

_____

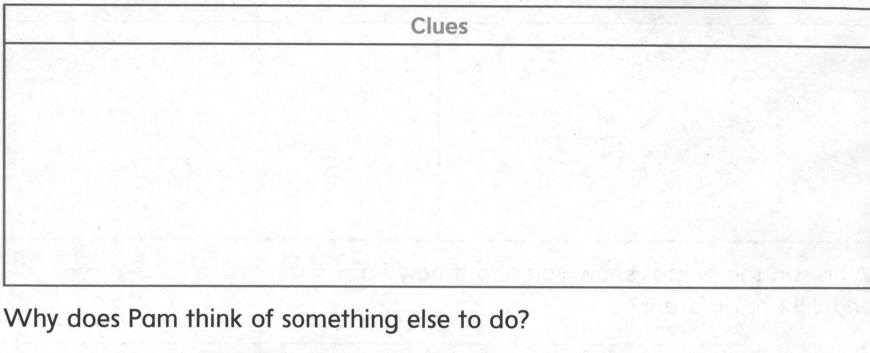

Write About It

How does Pam's plan change the way the girls play together?

"There Are Days and There Are Days"

 Share how the boy feels when he is alone.

Write three clues that help you understand how the boy feels when he is with a friend.

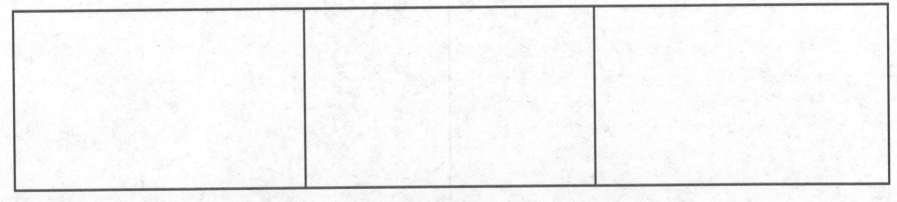

What do you notice about these words?
What feeling do you get from these words?

_____

_____

_____

_____

Quick Tip

Listen to the ending sounds in the words. What do you notice?

Talk about how you know the boys are friends.

Write about how the boy feels on pages 84 and 85. Reread the poem to help you.

Page 84	Pages 84-85

What do the words and picture show you about friends?

_____

- -

_____

- -

_____

Talk about what kinds of days there are for the boy.

 **Write** clues from the text that answer the questions.

Which words tell you about one kind of day?	Which words tell you about the other kind of day?

How does the boy feel about spending time with a friend?

_____

- -

_____

- -

_____

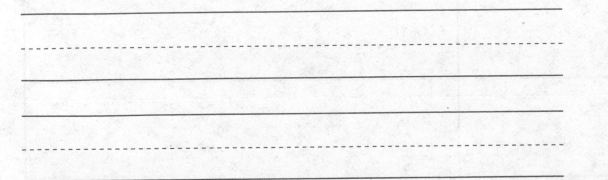

Talk About It

How does the poet help you know how the boy feels when he's alone and when he's with a friend?

Fun with Friends Poll

Step I Think about activities your classmates like to do with friends. Write five activities below.

Favorite Things to Do with Friends	Number of Children
1.	
2.	
3.	
4.	
5.	

Step 2 Ask your friends to take your poll.
Use the chart to tally the results.

Step 3 Think about the results of your poll.
What did you learn about your friends?

_____

_____

_____

_____

_____

_____

_____

_____

Step 4 Choose how to present your findings.

Talk about what the children in this painting are doing.

 Compare the children in the painting to Pam and Jill. How are they the same? How are they different?

Quick Tip

I can talk about the children using these sentence starters:

The children are . . .

They look . . .

The children play together.

What I Know Now

Think about the texts you heard and read this week about friends. Write what you learned.

_____

- -

_____

- -

_____

- -

_____

 Think about what else you would like to learn about friends. Talk about your ideas.

 Share one thing you learned this week about nonfiction texts.

Talk About It

? Essential Question **How does your body move?**

Talk and ask questions about how these kids are using their bodies.

 Write about or **draw** one way that you use your body.

Shared Read

(tcl): language from the credits: Juniors Bildarchiv GmbH/Alamy Stock Photo; (cl): language from the credits: McGraw-Hill Education/Ken Karp; (cr): language from the credits: RubberBall Productions/Photodisc/Getty Images

Find Text Evidence

Ask any questions you may have about the text. Read to find the answer.

Point to each word in the title as you read it.

Essential Question

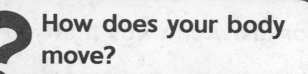

How does your body move?

Move and Grin!

Shared Read

 Underline and read aloud the words *jump* and *move*.

👥 Ask any questions you may have about the text. Read to find the answer.

Scott's frog can hop and jump.

It can move its back legs.

Scott can hop and jump, too.

Scott can hop, hop, hop.

Robert Daly/OJO Images/Getty Images

Read

Shared Read

🔍 **Find Text Evidence**

✏️ Circle and read aloud the words with the beginning sounds in *frog*.

✏️ Underline and read aloud the word *two*.

Fran's dog can swim a lot.

It kicks its two front legs.

Fran can swim a lot, too.

Fran can swim, swim, swim.

🔍 **Find Text Evidence**

 Circle and read aloud the words with the beginning sounds in *still*.

 Underline and read aloud the word *run*.

Stan's horse can trot and run.

It trots on its big legs.

Stan can trot, too.

Stan can trot, trot, trot.

Find Text Evidence

 Ask any other questions you have. Reread to find the answers.

Retell the text using the photos.

Skip's crab can grab.

It can grab with its big claw.

Grab, grab, grab.

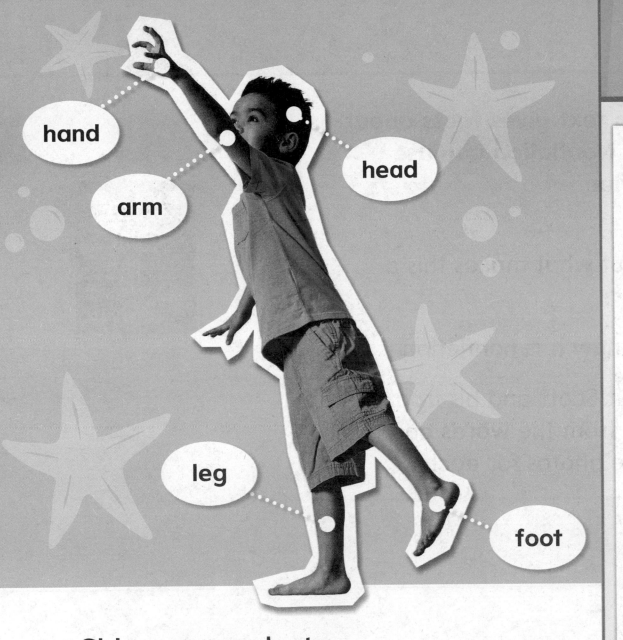

hand

arm

head

leg

foot

Skip can grab, too.

Skip can grab, grab, grab.

What can Skip grab with?

Remember, a nonfiction text gives facts about real people and things. Nonfiction can use photos to give information.

 Reread to find out what makes this a nonfiction text.

 Share how you know it is nonfiction.

Write facts about Scott and his frog. Include one fact from the words and one fact from the photos for each.

Facts about Scott	Facts about Scott's Frog

Skttoan
Pajt.

Frog can
Skttt Hop.

Remember, **key details** tell the most important information about the text. Words and photos can give you key details.

 Reread "Move and Grin!"

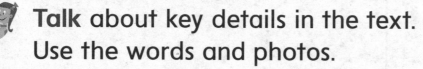 **Talk** about key details in the text. Use the words and photos.

 Write key details about how each animal and child can move.

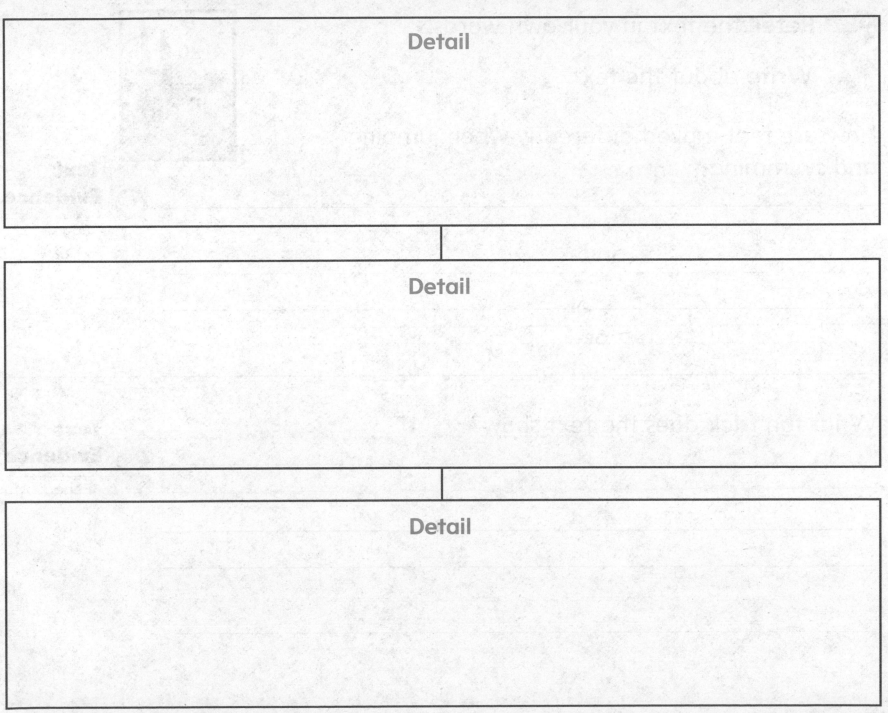

Detail

Detail

Detail

Retell the text in your own words.

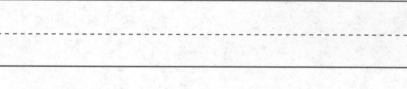 **Write** about the text.

Move It!

How are feet moved differently when jumping and swimming?

Text Evidence

Page

_____

_____

_____

What fun trick does the text show?

Text Evidence

Page

_____

_____

_____

Talk about how the texts are the same and different.

 Write about the texts.

What do both texts give information about?

_____

- -

_____

- -

_____

Which is your favorite way to move?

_____

- -

_____

- -

 **Make Inferences**

Use details to figure out things that are not stated.

Both texts show how children . . .

Talk about how the children move on pages 88–89.

 Write clues that help you know how the children jump and catch.

Jump	
Catch	

How does the author tell you how the children move?

_____

_____

_____

Talk about how you know how the boy moves on page 90.

 Write clues from the labels and photos to tell how the boy moves.

What does the boy use to swim?	How does he move them?

How do the labels and photo help you understand how the boy swims?

_____

_____

_____

Write About It

Describe the steps needed to make one of the motions in *Move It!*

My Family Hike

My name is Otto. Today I will look for snakes. We drive to the trail. My sister and I want to be first. I **start** to look for snakes.

Read to find out what happens on a family hike.

Underline the words that tell you Otto is telling his own story.

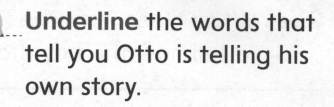

I see a snake! It hides. Finally we stop. We made it to the top of the mountain! I will look for **another** snake!

 Circle the clues that help you know how Otto feels. Talk about how he feels.

 Talk about why the word *another* is in bold print.

Write About It

Write about an important event in your life.

Include your feelings about the event.

How We Move in Sports

Step 1 **Choose** a sport to find out about.

_____

- -

_____

Step 2 **Decide** where to find information you need about the sport. Use titles to choose your books.

Step 3 **Write** facts about the sport.

_____

- -

_____

_____

- -

_____

- -

_____

Step 4 **Draw** and label the body parts used in your sport.

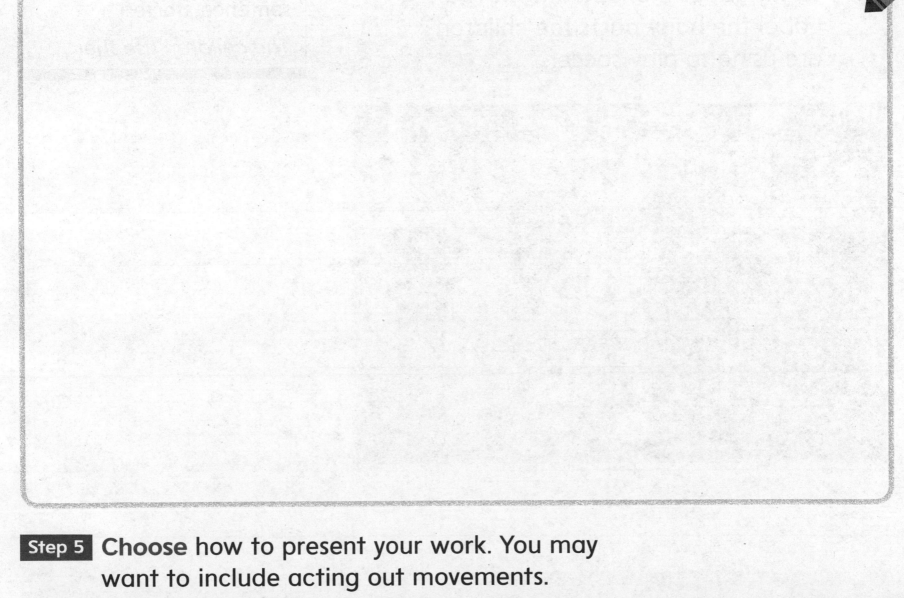

Step 5 **Choose** how to present your work. You may want to include acting out movements.

Talk about how the children in the photo are using their bodies.

Think about the labels in *Move It!* Label the body parts the children are using to play soccer.

What I Know Now

Think about the texts you heard and read this week about how bodies move. Write what you learned.

_____

- -

_____

- -

_____

- -

_____

- -

_____

 Talk about what else you would like to learn about how bodies move.

 Share one thing you learned this week about nonfiction texts.

Writing and Grammar

> I wrote a personal narrative. It tells something about me and includes the words *I*, *me*, and *my*.

Marisol

Personal Narrative

My personal narrative tells about something that happened to me.

Student Model

I Can Swim!

My name is Marisol.

Today my Aunt Rosa took me swimming.

First I was scared.

Then Aunt Rosa blew bubbles like a fish.

It looked like fun, so I jumped right in!

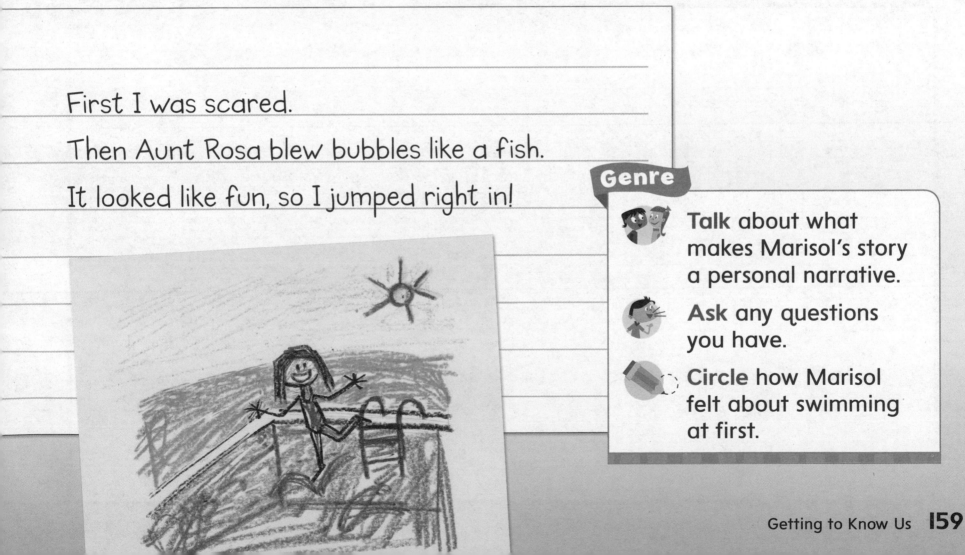

Genre

Talk about what makes Marisol's story a personal narrative.

Ask any questions you have.

Circle how Marisol felt about swimming at first.

Plan

 Talk about something that happened to you.

 Draw or write about what happened.

Quick Tip

Think about events that are important to you.

Choose something to write about.

_____

_____

_____

Write details about what happened.

_____

_____

_____

_____

_____

Circle what makes your story a personal narrative.

Draft

Read Marisol's draft of her personal narrative.

Student Model

My Special Day

My name is Marisol.

Today my Aunt Rosa took me swimming.

Key Details

I included an important detail to tell about what happened.

Ideas

I included a supporting detail to tell more about the event.

First I was scared.

Then Aunt Rosa blew bubbles.

It looked like fun, so I jumped right in!

Your Turn

Write your personal narrative in your writer's notebook. Use your ideas from pages 160–161. Include supporting details.

Revise and Edit

Think about how Marisol revised and edited her personal narrative.

I revised the title to tell more about my personal narrative.

I made sure to end each statement with a period.

Student Model

I Can Swim!

My name is Marisol.

Today my Aunt Rosa took me swimming.

I made sure to capitalize the first word in the sentence.

I added a key detail to make my writing more interesting.

First I was scared.

Then Aunt Rosa blew bubbles ʌlike a fish.

It looked like fun, so I jumped right in!

Grammar

- A sentence tells a whole idea. It ends with a period, a question mark, or an exclamation mark.

- A statement tells something.

- A question asks something.

- An exclamation shows strong feeling.

Your Turn

Revise and edit your writing in your writer's notebook. Use your checklist. Be sure to write complete sentences, including capital letters and punctuation.

Publish

 Finish editing your writing. Make sure it is neat and ready to publish.

 Practice presenting your work with a partner. Use this checklist.

 Present your work.

Review Your Work	Yes	No
Writing		
I wrote a personal narrative.	☐	☐
I included supporting details.	☐	☐
Speaking and Listening		
I introduced myself.	☐	☐
I spoke clearly.	☐	☐
I listened carefully.	☐	☐

Talk about what you did well in your writing.

Write about your work.

What did you do well in your writing?

_____

- -

_____

_____

- -

_____

What do you need to work on?

_____

- -

_____

_____

- -

_____

⟳ Spiral Review

Genre:
- Fantasy
- Nonfiction

Strategy:
- Visualize, Ask and Answer Questions

Skill:
- Key Details

Read "Sad Fran, Glad Fran." Picture the story in your mind as you read.

Sad Fran, Glad Fran

Fran Fox hops.
Fran slips!
Fran is sad!

Fran can not play.
Fran sits still.
It is not fun!

Rap! Rap! Rap!
It is Fran's pal
Dan Dog.
Fran is glad!

Fran and Dan play.
It is fun!

Show What You Learned

 Circle the correct answer to each question.

1 How can you tell the story is a fantasy?

   A Foxes like to move.

   B Fran lives in a house.

   C Fran has legs.

2 First, Fran Fox _____

   A jumps and runs.

   B has to stay in.

   C hops and slips.

3 What does Dan Dog do?

   A He breaks his leg.

   B He plays with Fran.

   C He reads a book with Fran.

> **Quick Tip**
>
> A fantasy is a made-up story.
>
> *A fantasy has characters who . . .*
>
> *A fantasy has events that . . .*

Look at the photos in "Move at School."

 Think of a question. Look for the answer as you read.

Move at School

Kids can be fit, fit, fit.
Kids can be fit at school.

Kids can hop, hop, hop.
Kids can skip, skip, skip.
Kids can jog, jog, jog.

(B)andresr/E+/Getty Images; (T)FatCamera/iStock/Getty Images

It is fun to move.
It is good for kids too.
It is **not** good to sit, sit, sit.

Kids move.
Kids do a good job in class.

Kids can be fit, fit, fit!

Circle the correct answer to each question.

1 How do you know this is a nonfiction text?

A It gives facts about kids.
B It does not give information.
C It is a made-up story about a kid.

2 Why should kids move at school?

A It helps them sleep.
B It makes them want to eat.
C It is fun and good for them.

3 Kids can get fit when they _____

A sit.
B hop.
C think.

Quick Tip

Look at the photos to find details that help you finish the sentence.

Focus on Fables

Fable is a genre. A fable is a made-up story that teaches a lesson. The characters are usually animals.

 Listen to "City Mouse and Country Mouse."

 Talk about the characters. What did they find out when they left home?

Write or **draw** what the country mouse learned.

Share the lesson you think this fable teaches.

Respond to the Read Aloud

A **diagram** can help you find and learn information.

 Look at the diagram as you listen to "Let's Move!"

 Talk about how the diagram helps you understand how the girl moves.

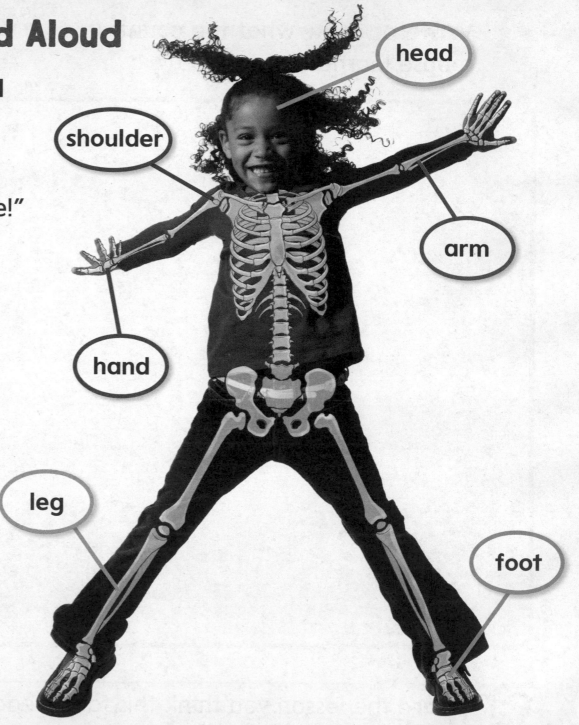

head

shoulder

arm

hand

leg

foot

Pick a part labeled in the diagram. Write two ways you can use that body part.

Body Part	Two Ways to Use It

Expand Vocabulary

Position words tell where things are.

 Talk about the position words *up, down, on,* and *off.*

 Label the picture using each position word.

 Say each position word aloud.

Some other position words are in, out, above, and below.

 Look at the picture. Use position words to tell what you see.

 Label the picture using the position words.

Stay Safe!

Find out how to stay safe and healthy during science activities. First, choose a science activity to learn about.

 Share questions you have about the best way to stay safe when doing the activity.

 Use books or the internet to find answers. Write how to follow safety rules for your activity.

_____

- -

_____

- -

_____

Reading Digitally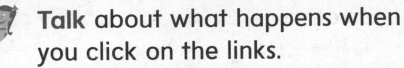

Online texts can have special features, such as **links**. Listen to "World Games" at <u>my.mheducation.com</u>. Click on the links.

 Talk about what happens when you click on the links.

Write what you learned.

_____

_____

_____

_____

_____

_____

Talk about what you learned.

Write a Personal Narrative

A **personal narrative** tells about an important event in your life. It can include the words *I, me, my,* and *we.*

 Look at and listen to this personal narrative.

The author chose an **event** in her life.

Details tell about what happened.

The author used the words **I** and **my**.

My Lost Tooth

At dinner today, we had corn on the cob. I took one bite and my front tooth fell out!

Now I can't eat corn, but I love my silly smile!

Talk about an important event in your life.

Write your personal narrative.

Choose Your Own Book

 Tell a partner about a book you want to read. Say why you want to read it.

 Write the title.

_____

- -

_____

 Write what you liked about the book.

Minutes I Read

_____

- -

_____

_____

- -

_____

Track Your Progress

What Did You Learn?

Think about the skills you have learned.
How happy are you with what you can do?

| I understand key details. | 🙂 | 😐 | ☹️ |

What is something that you want to get better at?

_____

- -

_____

- -

_____

- -

_____

My Sound-Spellings

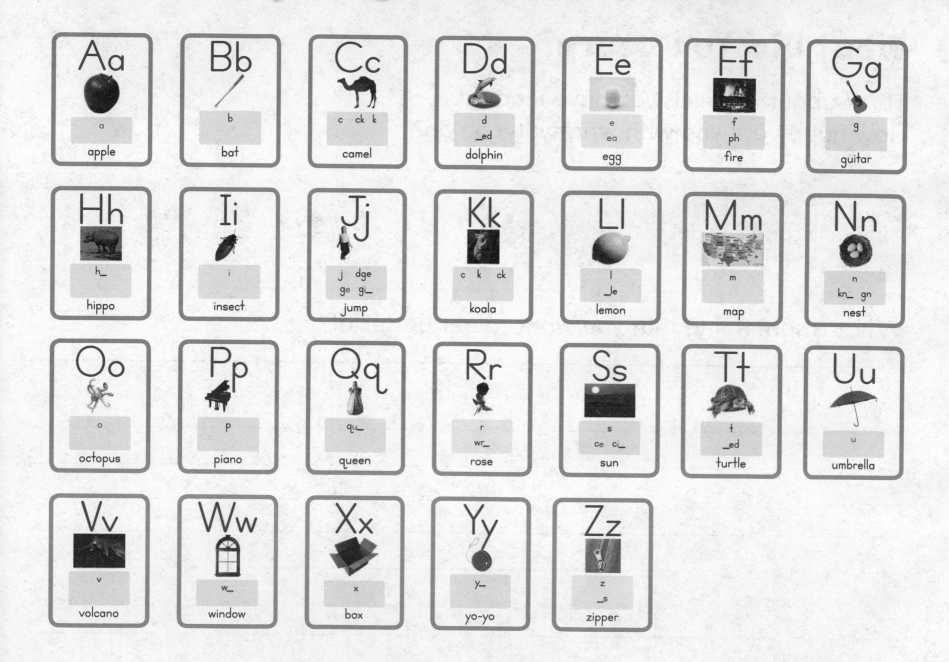

Aa apple — a	**Bb** bat — b	**Cc** camel — c ck k
Dd dolphin — d, _ed	**Ee** egg — e, ea	**Ff** fire — f, ph
Gg guitar — g		
Hh hippo — h_	**Ii** insect — i	**Jj** jump — j dge, ge gi_
Kk koala — c k ck	**Ll** lemon — l, _le	**Mm** map — m
Nn nest — n, kn_ gn		
Oo octopus — o	**Pp** piano — p	**Qq** queen — qu_
Rr rose — r, wr_	**Ss** sun — s, ce ci_	**Tt** turtle — t, _ed
Uu umbrella — u		
Vv volcano — v	**Ww** window — w_	**Xx** box — x
Yy yo-yo — y_	**Zz** zipper — z, _s	

Credits: (apple) Stockdisc/PunchStock; (bat) Radlund & Associates/Artville/Getty Images; (camel) Photodisc/Getty Images; (dolphin) imagebroker/Alamy; (egg) Pixtal/age fotostock; (fire) Comstock Images/Alamy; (guitar) Jules Frazier/Getty Images; (hippo) Michele Burgess/Corbis; (insect) Photodisc/Getty Images; (jump) Rubberball Productions/Getty Images; (koala) Al Franklin/Corbis; (lemon) C Squared Studios/Getty Images; (map) McGraw-Hill Education; (nest) Siede Preis/Photodisc/Getty Images; (octopus) Photographers Choice RF/SuperStock; (piano) Photo Spin/Getty Images; (queen) Joshua Ets-Hokin/Photodisc/Getty Images; (rose) Steve Cole/Photodisc/Getty Images; (sun) 97/E+/Getty Images; (turtle) Ingram Publishing/Fotosearch; (umbrella) Stockbyte/PunchStock; (volcano) Westend61/Getty Images; (window) Photodisc/Getty Images; (box) C Squared Studios/Getty Images; (yo-yo) D. Hurst/Alamy; (zipper) ImageState/Alamy

th thumb	sh shell	ch tch cheese	wh_ whale	ng sing	a ai_ _ay a_e ea ei train	i y i_e igh ie five
o oa ow o_e _oe boat	u u_e _ew _ue cube	e_e ea ee e _y ie _ey tree	ar star	er ir ur or shirt	oar or ore corn	ow ou cow
oi _oy boy	oo book	oo u_e u _ew ue ou ui spoon	a aw au augh al straw	air are ear ere chair		

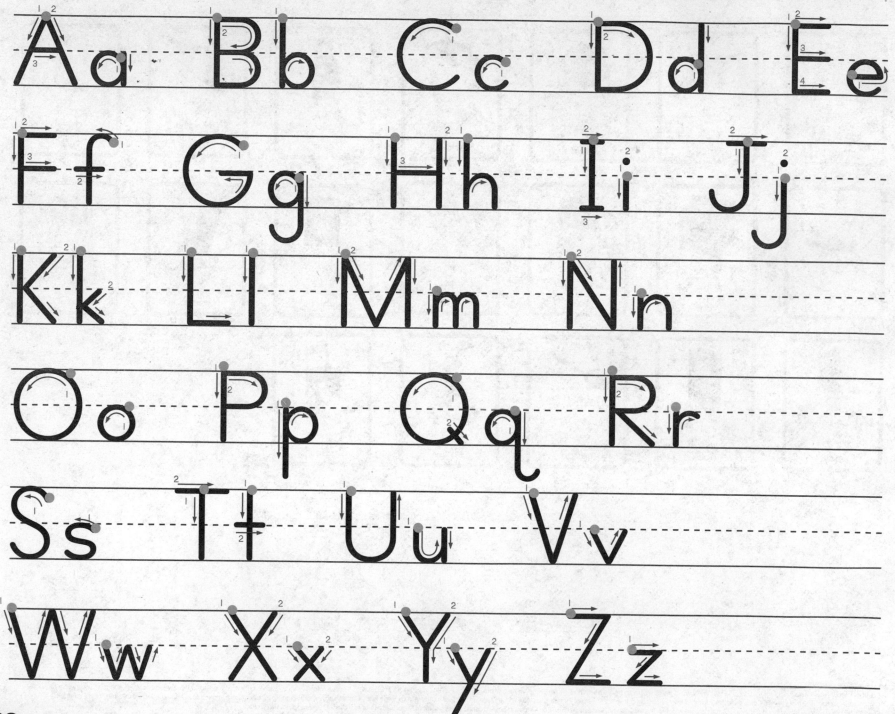

Aa Bb Cc Dd Ee
Ff Gg Hh Ii Jj
Kk Ll Mm Nn
Oo Pp Qq Rr
Ss Tt Uu Vv
Ww Xx Yy Zz....

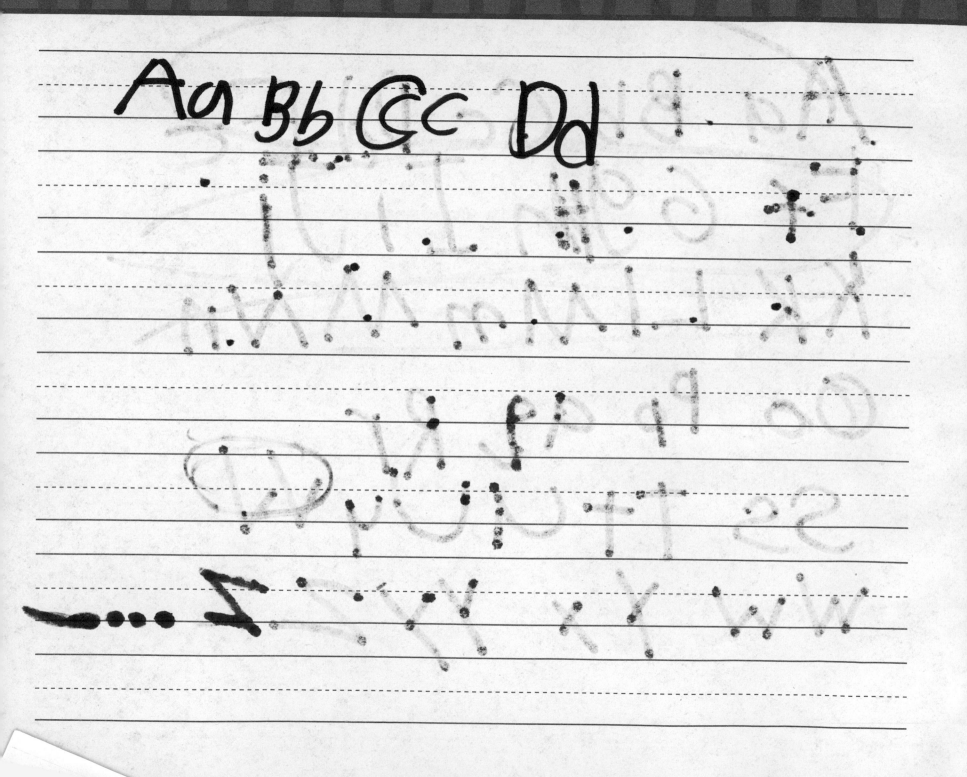

Aa Bb Ccc Dd